Fax-Ready GUERRILLA GRAMS

**Instant
Tear-Out,
Feed-In
Business Faxes
With A
Mission.**

Igor Faxemoff

4470-107 Sunset Blvd., Suite 234
Los Angeles, California 90027

Distributed by The Globe Pequot Press
P.O. Box 833, 6 Business Park Road
Old Saybrook, CT 06475-0833

Distributed in Canada by Thomas Allen & Son, Ltd.

Library of Congress Cataloging-in-Publication Data

Faxemoff, Igor.
    Fax-ready guerrilla grams : instant tear-out, feed in business faxes
  with a mission / Igor Faxemoff.
          p.   cm.
      ISBN 0-944042-29-5
      1. Commercial correspondence—Caricatures and cartoons.
  2. Facsimile transmission. I. CorkScrew Press. II. Title.
  III. Title: Guerrilla grams.
      HF5726.F39 1994   651.7'5—dc20   94-8683

For single-copy orders: see page 111. For quantity discounts and imprintings for sales promotions, premiums, fund-raising and educational uses, please write to the distributor.

Printed in the U.S.A.

10 9 8 7 6 5 4 3 2 1

Warning

You have in your hands
the single greatest advancement
in fax technology since the
invention of the fax itself.

Your fax machine's
untapped potential is
about to be unleashed.

It is now your very own
business assault weapon.

♦ Follow all directions carefully.

♦ Use your *Guerrilla Grams* wisely.

♦ And remember: use this power
for good — not for evil.

A Note From
Mr. Faxemoff

Of course it's not my real name. If I told you who I was, you'd call me to ask for something. Years ago, I learned the value of getting through to the right people. Now that I'm much too rich and busy to return *your* calls, I thought I'd pass along a secret to getting through to everyone on the planet...but me.

Enjoy this book. Use it to build bridges, not burn them.

Power to the faxor,

Igor

Igor Faxemoff

P.S. Do you need a *Guerrilla Gram* you didn't find here?

Send me your idea in care of the publisher and it could appear in the sequel: *Fax-Ready Guerrilla Grams — The Counterattack.*

Contents

For

*Everyone with a goal —
who has someone standing
in the way.*

Thank You

Joe Azar
Natalie Windsor
Donna Panullo
Lisa Beezley
Arthur Lampel
Rich Lippman
Steve Spar
Mike O'Brien
Neal Marks
Globe Pequot
Ro & Shel

Cover Design

Ken Niles
Ad Infinitum
Santa Monica, CA

How To Use This Book

Precisely what do you want? Money? Attention? Power? Relief? Gratitude? They're all in here.

Pick the *Guerrilla Grams* that convey your intention and intensity. Try to imagine your faxees' reactions *before* you fax. Leave room for negotiation. And then consider your timing: a message faxed at midnight not only makes you the first thing they see in the morning — it's also cheaper.

Use *Guerrilla Grams* to open doors, or as icebreaking tools to justify follow-up phone calls. Be ready — any message sent with one of these pages will get special attention and office buzz. However, if you're not sure about your faxees' sense of humor, assume they don't have one.

You are now empowered with the tools that bend people's wills to your own. They also work real well on bending rules. But before you touch that '*Send*' button, remember: what goes around comes around.

PRACTICE SAFE FAX: Your fax machine will put an ID line and phone number at the top of every sheet. If you want your *Guerrilla Gram* to be anonymous, check the instructions and wipe out that top line *before* you fax!

Guerrilla Grams begin on the next page.

Call Me

How many times are you willing to call without getting an answer?

What if they're not ignoring you — they just don't know you're there?

I'm stuck in your voice mail

and I can't get out.

Won't YOU please call ME?

To _____

From _____ Phone ( ) _____

Call Me

You're perfectly willing to forgive them for not calling you back — but amnesty expires at close of business today.

Thanks!

Check off credit where credit is due. Make sure they'll be there for you next time, too.

Thanks!
YOU SAVED MY
- DAY.
- JOB.
- LIFE.
- REPUTATION.
- BEHIND.

To _____

From _____

YOU'VE JUST BEEN HIT WITH A *FAX-READY GUERRILLA GRAM*   © CorkScrew Press

Thanks!

Lunch on me.
To _Linda_
From _Igor_

This is the way the best business is done. It'll never again be *this* easy to show your appreciation.

Allow me to show my appreciation...

Lunch on me.

To _____

From _____

Thanks!

People don't say this enough. To be really successful, use this four times a day.

I'm telling the whole world how grateful I am.

And you can't stop me.

To _____ From _____

Thanks!

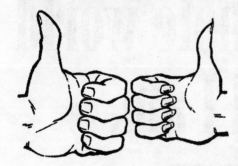 Got the promotion? Made the sale? Won the account? Show your support for the people who support you. Let 'em have it.

Thanks for the vote of confidence!

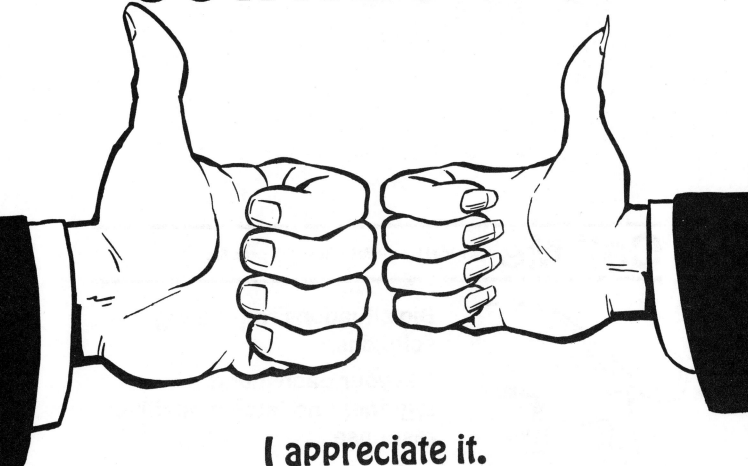

I appreciate it.

To _____ From _____

Call Me

Special 2-page fax — feed this page first.

Big situations require big solutions.

Get your dachshund together and fetch a positive response.

Instructions: Tape the next two pages end-to-end and feed it through as one long fax.

20

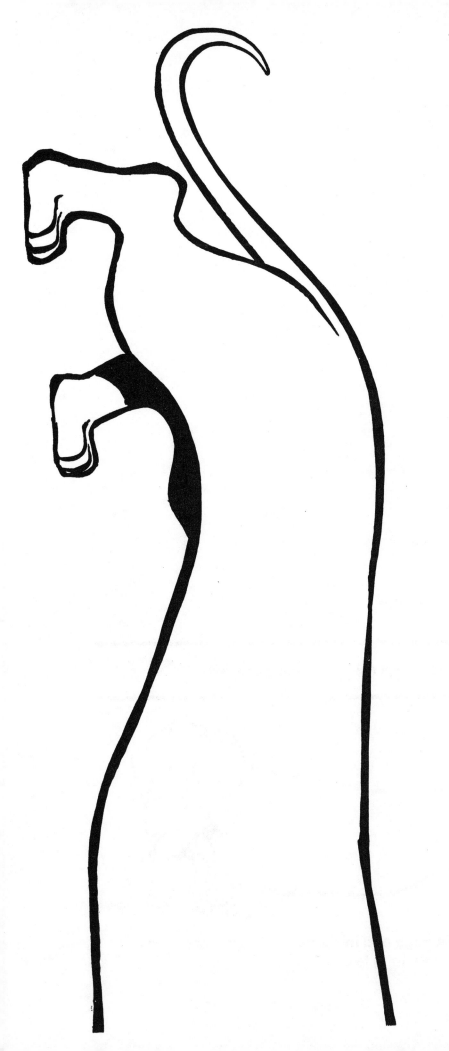

Please call me right away ...

To _____

Call Me

Special 2-page fax — feed this page last.

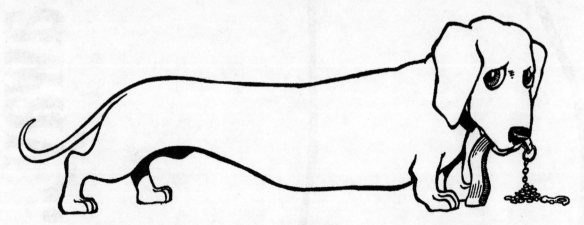

Instructions: Tape this page and the previous page end-to-end and feed it through as one long fax.

...I have to go out!!!

From

Thanks.

YOU'VE JUST BEEN HIT WITH A *FAX-READY GUERRILLA GRAM* © CorkScrew Press

Call Me

Are they playing duck and cover with you? This should flush 'em out.

Where the heck are you?

Last chance to call before I take it personally.

To _____ From _____ at ( ) _____

Call Me

It's getting serious...

Fax this, before you get your
cold wet nose outta joint.

I only know one more way to track you down:

To _____

Please call me right away at

(   ) _____

and I'll stop hounding you.

From _____

Call Me

Even if you think they're avoiding you, give 'em enough slack to call you back.

28

Are You Hung Up?

Please don't hang <u>me</u> up.
Call already!

To _____ From _____

My phone number is (   ) _____ ext. _____

Thank you.

Pay Me

They're nice. You're nice.
Just a little friendly nudge to keep it that way.

How about giving it a happy ending?

And the nice people paid their bill *in full* ...

And everyone lived happily ever after.

To _____

From _____

Pay Me

For delinquent accounts with a sense of humor and a respect for classic movies.

If they won't pay you out of fairness, let 'em pay you out of fear.

I'LL GET YOU, MY PRETTY

AND YOUR LATE CHARGES, TOO!

TO _____

FROM _____

Prevent flying monkeys. Pay your bill.

Pay Me

For good accounts going through bad times.

Don't rub it in if you think this is the only one of these they've seen in a while.

Do you have this in green?

Your account is late. Please check your records.

To _____ From _____

Pay Me

Funny or grim, depending on the size of their outstanding balance.

Our C.F.O. wants to know

why
you
haven't
paid
your
bill.

To_____ From _____ at ( ) _____

Maneuvering Room

They got you, and they're right.

Let them know your intentions are good, even if your bank balance isn't.

Call Off Your Dogs.

The check will soon
be on its way.
Thanks for your patience.

To _____ From _____

Maneuvering room

 For nagging creditors and persistent collection agencies who need to know you're an *honorable* deadbeat.

When I Get Mine...

You Get Yours.

To _____ From _____

Call me

You jumped through hoops to get your proposal in, only to wait forever for a reply. This should get your hoops up.

Can I Exhale Yet?

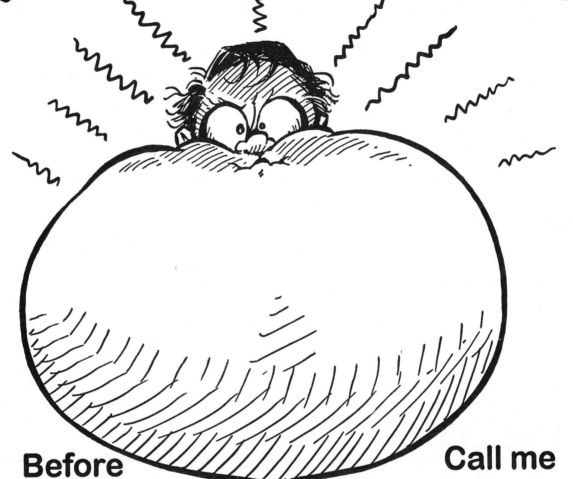

Before
I explode...

Call me
with your
answer!

To _____

Regarding _____

From _____ Phone ( ) _____

Get real

Designed for junk faxers or good friends with bad suggestions.

THANK YOU FOR YOUR RECENT FAX.

It's been forwarded to the appropriate department.

Get a clue

They think they just faxed to the right person.

Let 'em know they're all faxed up.

WE JUST GOT YOUR FAX.

WHO ON EARTH ARE YOU?

Check the number and fax it again — to the correct humanoid.

Fax again

The part that came through makes you hunger for the rest of it. Use this to tell 'em they're only half-faxed.

Get a clue

For chilling out Romeos and wising up blabber-faxers. Really, it's kinder to tell 'em *before* secrets fall into enemy hands.

Everyone here can't wait for your next fax.

Cut out the personal stuff.
This is a place of business.

To _____

Get real

Cut the boneheads off — before the boss sees what's comin' through the fax machine.

This is a place of business.

Your fax was inappropriate.

To _____ From _____

Get a clue

If they won't respect your privacy out of a sense of fair play — hit 'em with fear.

Warning: This is your trump card. Use only in ultimate cases.

D.L. BEEZLEY
ARNOLD BECKER
IGOR FAXEMOFF
JOYCE DAVENPORT
HAMILTON BURGER
VICTOR SIFUENTES
CLINTON JUDD
LAWRENCE PRESTON
PERRY MASON
JONATHAN ROLLINS
MICHAEL KUZAK
ANN KELSEY
GRACE VAN OWEN

BEEZLEY, BECKER & FAXEMOFF

A PROFESSIONAL CORPORATION

ATTORNEYS AT LAW

4800 NATIONAL BANK TOWER EAST
1280 AVENUE OF THE AMERICAS
60TH FLOOR
NEW YORK, NEW YORK 10020
(212) 555-9000

TELECOPIER
(212) 555-9833

TELECOPIER COVER LETTER

PLEASE DELIVER THE FOLLOWING PAGES TO:

NAME: _____

SENDER: Igor Faxemoff OF BEEZLEY, BECKER & FAXEMOFF

DATE SENT: _____ 19___ TIME: _____

THIS TELECOPY CONSISTS OF -01- PAGE(S), INCLUDING THIS COVER
SHEET. IF YOU DO NOT RECEIVE ALL OF THE PAGES, PLEASE
TELEPHONE BEEZLEY, BECKER & FAXEMOFF IMMEDIATELY.

MESSAGE:

> **YOUR PREVIOUS FACSIMILE IS BEING RETAINED AS EVIDENCE.
> CEASE FURTHER COMMUNICATION IMMEDIATELY.**
>
> Igor Faxemoff

FOR BEEZLEY, BECKER & FAXEMOFF USE ONLY:
FILE NUMBER: X493D GF93D Y   DOCUMENT: WP/LP.WPD   EDE 432

YOU'VE JUST BEEN HIT WITH A *FAX-READY GUERRILLA GRAM*   © CorkScrew Press

Get real

How do *you* spell relief?

They may not know they're choking you unless you tell them. Check one.

56

I'm really starting to feel

Please revise your:

☐ estimate.
☐ deadline.
☐ goals.
☐ expectations.
☐ _____.

To _____ From _____

© CorkScrew Press

Brace yourself

Putting this sheet in front of your suggested changes won't lighten their workload, but it might soften the blow.

Dear _____,

I'm sure you don't want to hear this

BUT,

there's
one
more
change.

Sheepishly, _____

____ pages to follow

Call me

If technology's ever fouled you up, here's your chance to make it work *for* you.

C O V E R S H E E T

FAX

To _____

From _____

Date _____ Number of pages _____

If you do not receive this entire fax transmission, please call the sender immediately at (   ) _____

MESSAGE:

GREAT NEWS!!! I tried and tried to get through to you on the phone. You're really going to be THRILLED. So call me right away so I can give you all the details about how

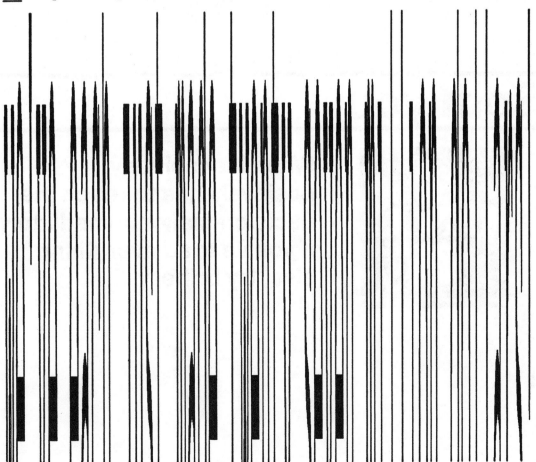

Spiff you

When it absolutely, positively has to reach the decision-maker immediately. If you've tried everything else, try bribery.

Dear _____,

Please hand-deliver the following ___ pages right away to:

_____

and redeem this valuable coupon for:

ONE
Medium-Sized Favor

X _____
Signature

FAVOR MUST BE WITHIN REASON, AND MEDIUM SIZED. SOME RESTRICTIONS APPLY. NO EXPIRATION DATE. COUPON MAY NOT BE COMBINED WITH ANY OTHER OFFERS, NOR ASSIGNED TO A THIRD PARTY. VOID WHERE PROHIBITED BY LAW. ANY AND ALL TAXES ARE THE SOLE RESPONSIBILITY OF THE WINNER. YOUR GAS MILEAGE MAY VARY. OBJECTS IN MIRROR MAY BE CLOSER THEN THEY APPEAR. MEMBER FSLIC.

Move it or lose it

SORRY— WILL TRY TO ORDER TROPHY TOMORROW. —AL

Sure they're late, but this friendly fax from 'Al' could get them to come through.

CONGRATULATIONS!

To _____

You are a finalist for the prestigious

AL DEWITT TAMARA AWARD

Presented by the American Society of Aspiring Procrastinators

Move it or lose it

You're late, but if you fax them you might still save the project.

Sorry it's late.

Would you believe...?

To _____,

Please believe you'll have it by _____

Yours truly, _____

Empathy & Compassion

Sure they're not coughing on you — but they're probably infecting the entire office. A little advice goes a long way.

NINE OUT OF TEN DOCTORS AGREE.

You're indespensible — but go home and rest anyway.

To _____ From _____

Hope you feel better soon.

Rain check

Can't make the appointment but too chicken to call? One fax says it all.

I'm swamped.

Sorry, but I'm too dam busy.
I'll call you to reschedule.

To _____

From _____ Phone (___) _____

24-hour pass

Sincerely,
Igor's Mom

Heck, it's worth a try.

A message from Mom

Dear _____,

My ☐ son
☐ daughter will not be coming
to work today because ☐ he
is home with: ☐ she

☐ a headache
☐ a tummy ache
☐ ~~dirahear~~ diharera
☐ the flu that's going around
☐ a bad haircut
☐ you really don't wanna know.

Sincerely,

_____'s Mom

P.S. This time it's for real.

Uh Oh.

Not what you expected. Would some good-humored preventive maintenance nip this in the bud?

Your suggestion has opened more than our eyes...

Now what?

To _____ From _____

Number of pages following _____

Uh Oh.

Not what you expected.
Big problems. Buy some
time while you squeegee
the walls.

I'LL GET BACK TO YOU LATER

SOMETHING JUST HIT THE FAN

To _____

From _____

Uh Oh.

Don't even ask. You'll know when you need this one.

Don't Panic.

I'm working on it...you'll have it soon.
Promise!

To _____ **From** _____

Take notice

To separate your memo from the other stuff on their desks, carve it in stone and deliver it from on high.

A Commandment From
THE BOSS:

Thou Shalt Not Ignore.

Nail it down

You trust them. They trust you. A little ink now will preserve a lot later.

Let's cement our agreement in writing.

To _____ From _____

Heads up

Be there, or be volunteered to head another four committees.

Don't be late for our conference call

or we'll talk about you.

Date_____ Our Time _____ Your Time _____

With _____

_____

Regarding _____

Parlez-vous fax?

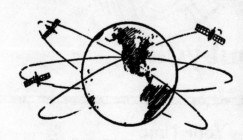 **It may take seconds to get that message half-way around the globe, into the hands of a local who'll take days to deliver it.**

International Fax

C O V E R   S H E E T

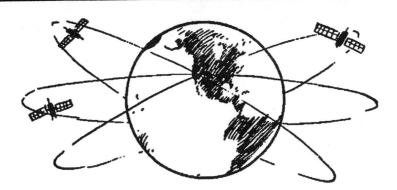

Please deliver immediately.
Délivrez immédiatement, s'il vous plaît.
Entregue inmediatamente, por favor.
Recapitare subito, per favore.
Übergeben Sie bitte sofort.
Overlämna genast, var så god.
נא להעביר מיד.
スグ オクハ゜リクタ゜ サイ
Передайте сразу, пожалуйста
Παραδῶστε αμέσως, παρακαλῶ

To _____ Company _____

Hotel _____

From _____ Company_____

Number of pages to follow _____

Problem? Problème? Problema? Probleme?
בעיה? モンダ゜ イ? Πρώβλημα; Проблема?

Country code _____ Phone ( ) _____

☐ Confidential. Confidentiel. Confidencial. Riservato. Förtrolig. Vertraulich.
סודי. Εμπιστευτικό. Конфиденциально. シンテン。

Way to go

 A trip in a nutshell. For yourself, your boss, or the welcoming committee.

ITINERARY

To _____

From _____

DEPARTURE

Date _____ Time _____

City/Airport _____

Airline _____ Flight _____

Connecting flight(s) _____

ARRIVAL

Airport _____

Time _____ ❑ am ❑ pm

GROUND TRANSPORTATION

❑ I'm renting a car   ❑ Taking a cab
❑ You're picking me up

ACCOMMODATIONS

Hotel _____

Phone _____ Fax _____

RETURN

Date _____

Airport _____

Time _____

Airline/Flight _____

Flight _____

Way to go

If you can't be the one going, you might as well *look* gracious.

Enjoy your vacation!

Relax all you can —
no one's gonna do your work
while you're gone!

To _____   From _____

Party!

Just remember — a posted fax could mean you'll need lots more snacks when the whole company shows up!

If you missed our last party...

You won't want to miss this one:

Occasion_____

Where _____

When _____**Time** _____

Future VP

 **Too busy to call? One fax does it all.**

IT'S A TAX DEDUCTION!

□ Boy □ Girl   Name _____

Parents _____

Date of Birth _____ Time _____

Weight _____ Length _____

Office Pool Winner _____

Top secret

From tax returns to love notes, sooner or later you're gonna hafta fax something you'd rather keep private. Cover that bet with a little intimidation.

C O V E R   S H E E T

PRIVILEGED & CONFIDENTIAL

TO _____

FROM _____

NUMBER OF PAGES _____

If you're not the person named above, you've read too much already. Just hand this entire fax to its intended recipient and nobody'll get hurt.

Special effax

Sure you can fax it in no time, but who knows how long before some low-life flunky delivers it? Increase your odds with a little urgency.

To _____

From _____

Date _____

Number of pages following _____

Special effax

Just because they fax it, they assume you sit by the machine all day, ready to respond at a moment's notice. Show 'em they're right.

Special effax

When civilization as we know it depends on your fax.

COVER SHEET

This Fax Rated:

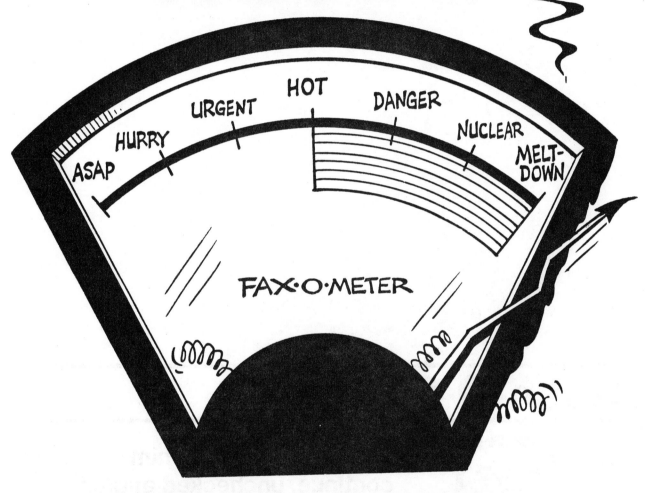

Handle with utter immediacy.

To _____ From _____

Date _____ Number of pages following _____

Action:

YOU'VE JUST BEEN HIT WITH A *FAX-READY GUERRILLA GRAM* © CorkScrew Press

Rush-O-Gram

Are you going to let him continue, unchecked and/or unrewarded? You know where he stands — tell him where *you* stand.

Last known fax number: 212/563-9166.

Rush-O-Gram

Dear Rush,

Absolutely sincerely,

_____

Stern-O-Gram

Are you going to let him continue, unchecked and/or unrewarded? You know where he stands — tell him where *you* stand.

Last known fax number: 212/759-5329.

STERN-O-GRAM

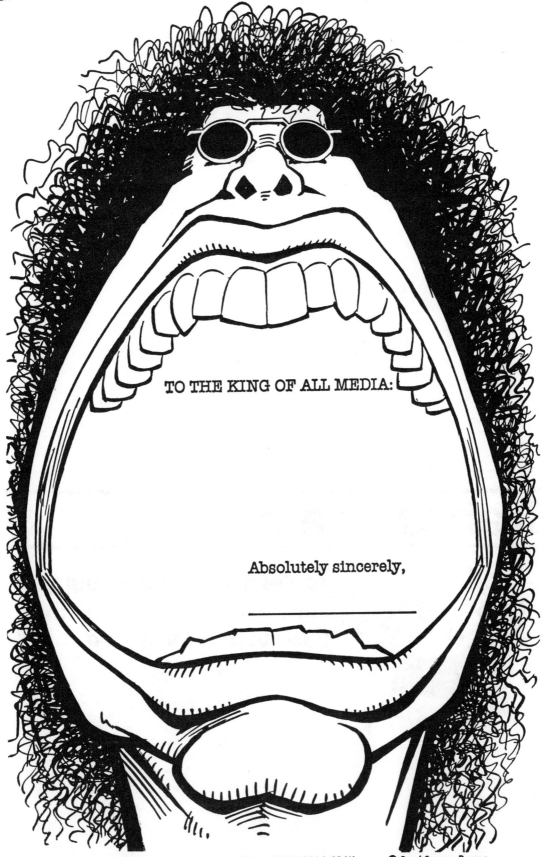

TO THE KING OF ALL MEDIA:

Absolutely sincerely,

_____

Crab-O-Gram

You're mad as heck, but you still have to take it. So fill this out and pass it on.

Crab-O-Gram

To _____

Here's what's makin' ME crabby:

➤ Meetings at 4:45.

➤ Putting on the coffee, answering the phone, and coming back to find the pot already empty.

➤ Consultants who get paid big bucks to tell the boss what you suggested six months ago.

➤ The copier's down. Again.

➤ State-of-the-art equipment you have no idea how to use.

➤ Sniffling, sneezing co-workers who borrow your phone.

➤ "Everybody, meet your new supervisor."

➤ Your competition for the promotion is the boss's nephew.

➤ Finding out your big new raise nets you $6.41 a week after taxes.

➤ _____
_____
_____!

From _____

Make my day

If you like what we did for your fax machine, wait'll you see what we can do for all your major appliances!

More fun by fax!

CorkScrew Press has a book for every mood, attitude and gift-giving occasion.

Order by fax, phone or mail. Or visit your bookstore. Why stop the fun just because you've reached the end of *this* book?

How many?

☐ **EATING IN — The Official Single Man's Cookbook**

Look like Paul Newman in the kitchen with this funny, illustrated step-by-step guide to better dating through cooking. Only $8.95

☐ **"IT WAS ON FIRE WHEN I LAST CHECKED ON IT"**
The Easy Cookbook for Busy Women

An ideal gift for the woman who wants good food fast — not fast food! Only $8.95

☐ **FAX-READY GUERRILLA GRAMS** $8.95

You're holdin' it. You still need a description?

☐ **1,000,001 THINGS THAT MAKE YOU CRABBY**

The only truly funny collection of universal steam venters. Open it anywhere and within a split-second, you're laughing. Only $6.95

☐ **HOW TO FLY — *Relaxed & Happy From Takeoff to Touchdown***

The carry-on airplane companion to make your flights safer, calmer, happier. Only $5.95

☐ **THE SMARTEST, SMALLEST, SAVVIEST BOOK OF TRAVEL SECRETS**

Travel like a pro — skip the scams, maximize your money and pack the most fun into your trip. $6.95

10-Day Money-Back Guarantee!

➤ **Fax this entire form — day or night: (203) 395-0312**
➤ **Call toll-free: 1-800-243-0495 (CT only: 1-800-962-0973)**
➤ **Order by mail: PO Box 833 • Old Saybrook, CT 06475-0833**

Name _____

Address _____

_____

City/State/Zip _____

Total cost of books ordered $_____

CT addresses add 6% sales tax _____

Add $3 per book s&h _____

TOTAL ENCLOSED $_____
Thank you!

Charge It!

☐ **Please charge my ☐ MasterCard ☐ VISA**

Card number _____

Expiration date _____

Signature _____

☐ *For mail orders only:*
I've enclosed a ☐ check ☐ money order payable to: *Globe Pequot Press*

In a Big Hurry??

One- or two-day *RUSH* service is available for a small extra charge — call 1-800-243-0495. Otherwise, please allow up to 2 weeks for delivery.